AUSTRALIAN
ABORIGINAL RELIGION

FASCICLE THREE

INSTITUTE OF RELIGIOUS ICONOGRAPHY
STATE UNIVERSITY GRONINGEN

ICONOGRAPHY OF RELIGIONS

EDITED BY

TH. P. VAN BAAREN, L. LEERTOUWER and H. BUNING (*Secretary*)

SECTION V: AUSTRALIAN ABORIGINAL RELIGION

FASCICLE THREE

LEIDEN
E. J. BRILL
1974

AUSTRALIAN ABORIGINAL RELIGION

BY

RONALD M. BERNDT

FASCICLE THREE
NORTH AUSTRALIA (*continued*)

With 40 Plates

LEIDEN
E. J. BRILL
1974

This Section consists of four Fascicles

ISBN 90 04 03727 6

CONTENTS

The Map to Chapter Four (*continued*) will be found in Fascicle Two, at the end

READERS IN AUSTRALIA PLEASE NOTE:

This work is a serious anthropological study of Australian Aboriginal religion. It is designed to be read by adults, and is primarily for use in universities and/or similar institutions. It is not, therefore, for use in schools.

Where Australian Aborigines are concerned, and in areas where traditional Aboriginal religion is still significant, this book should be used only after consultation with local male religious leaders.

This restriction is important. It is imposed because the concept of what is secret, or may not be revealed to the uninitiated in Aboriginal religious belief and action, varies considerably throughout the Australian continent; and because the varying views of Aborigines in this respect must on all occasions be observed.

January 30th 1973   Ronald M. BERNDT

PREFACE

Fascicle Three continues the study of Australian Aboriginal religion.

Fascicles One and Two provided a general view of Aboriginal religion, dealing with the broad concepts upon which the empirical material in this Fascicle rests. Among these are the pervading influence of the Dreaming and of totemism, seen within their overall context, in an integrated view of religious belief and action. These Fascicles also considered traditional religious material in south-eastern and north-eastern Australia. They take into account variations and differences in general patterning. In the north-east, for instance, the religious emphasis is more directly of the northern Fertility type, although with quite pronounced undertones of Central Australian religious style.

The second Fascicle (Two) saw the commencement of our consideration of North Australian material. For publication reasons, this had to be divided into two, after discussion of death and its religious significance in relation to the life cycle. From that point we continue in this Fascicle (Three).

The core of this particular study of Aboriginal religion is actually the presentation of materials on North and Central Australia. This is mainly because the societies and cultures of those religions are 'living', or were so until quite recently: religion still means a great deal to the Aborigines concerned. Religious beliefs can be discussed in detail, with people who actually hold them—not as something which belongs to the past. Also, their ritual expressions (including iconographic aspects) are there to be seen in their traditional settings. This is especially important because in these circumstances we do not have to infer meanings, and gaps in our knowledge—anthropologically speaking—are not so apparent and can still be filled. The emergent material can be looked at from varying empirical angles: it is not already crystallized—or, alternatively, blurred—as has been the case in so many other areas where traditional life has disappeared, or has become a memory of the past lingering on in the minds of the aged, or used for new purposes in an entirely different and usually political context.

In discussing this 'live' material, I have chosen to look at it in the context of the life cycle of Aboriginal man. Religion concerns the progression of man through life crises. It is geared toward assisting him to cope with the problems of living; and this involves learning, acquiring (mostly, in an Aboriginal setting, through religious action) information and attitudes that he can apply in particular situations for purposes of survival—both physically and psycho-socially. Underpinning this is a three-fold relationship between man and his environment and all within it, and the supernatural forces which activate it. Man is seen as part of nature. The continuity of life is not something that commences with birth and ends inevitably with death: it is, rather, an open-ended continuum. The source of life is to be found in the Dreaming, and in the mythic beings who belong within it: death is simply a return to the Dreaming, with eventual opportunities for rebirth.

Aboriginal religion is life-minded and life-centred: even in mortuary rituals, the stress is on life. One of the most outstanding demonstrations of this is to be found in the Fertility

Cults which are considered in this Fascicle. These, within the framework of complementary relationships between males and females, express the importance of mythic creative Mothers. Up to the time Professor W. Lloyd Warner carried out research among the so-called 'Murngin' of north-eastern Arnhem Land in 1926-29, little reference had been made in the literature to such cults. They had been referred to by Sir Baldwin Spencer in his North Australian investigations, but never really considered seriously. In such circumstances, the 'typical' picture of Aboriginal religion was that provided by Durkheim, who based his study primarily on Central Australian data. These were in marked contrast to what was later reported from northern Aboriginal societies. It was not until the work of Professors A. P. Elkin and R. M. Berndt in the mid-forties that a clear view of the Fertility Cults emerged, and was later added to by Professors W. E. H. Stanner and M. Meggitt.

In this Fascicle, full bibliographical references appear for the whole of Chapter Four of this study. Iconographically, this is the richest of all Aboriginal regions.

Department of Anthropology,   Ronald M. BERNDT
University of Western Australia

NORTH AUSTRALIA

This discussion of Australian Aboriginal religion focuses on religion and the life cycle and on the fertility cults. In the previous fascicle, the subjects of birth and death were considered along with initiation rituals.

This fascicle completes Chapter Four of the study.

FERTILITY CULTS

It has been said that 'first initiation' is a ritual introduction to the Dreaming: in other words, for an Aboriginal man in particular, religious activities and duties commence at that time in earnest. The main concentration is on the well-being of the person and the social group in which he lives: in short, the maintenance of the life he knows. There are two facets to this. One is the continuation of food resources, the other the continuation of human beings *per se*. In either case, ritual interpretations are not necessarily phrased directly in those terms. Symbolic patterning is often intricate and serves as an intermediary between the Dreaming and mundane existence. The Aborigines would undoubtedly have considered it improvident to leave nature to take its own course without some sort of intervention. The general belief is that it must be stimulated through the power inherent in the mythic beings—the power which, in the creative era, was responsible for activating nature, including man and the natural species. That which is natural (pertaining to nature) must be constantly renewed, in a continuing process on the theme of re-birth and/or revival. Just as an ordinary human birth cannot take place without spiritual animation, so the renewal of nature in its broadest sense requires spiritual activation: and this can be achieved only through ritual.

In this section, then, we consider some of the great fertility cults. These are not of predominantly local significance, tied to specific sites, but have spread across quite large areas. They are to be seen in contrast to isolated acts of increase and small tribally-bound rituals (see, for example, Elkin 1938/64: Chapter IX; R. and C. Berndt 1964/68: 227-31).

One of the most outstanding of these is the Djanggawul (Djanggau) myth-ritual complex of north-eastern Arnhem Land (R. Berndt 1952), first reported by Warner (1937/58: 335-70). It belongs within the *dua* moiety, and the rites are called, collectively, the *dua nara*. The main characters are a Brother and his two Sisters (sometimes with a companion) who, in the *wongar* Dreaming era, travelled by bark canoe from Bralgu, the *dua* moiety Land of the Dead or land of the immortals. In some versions, the Sisters are said to be the Daughters of the Sun. Within the canoe were hidden various sacred objects, among them the *ngainmara* (*nganmara*) conical mat, a plaited dillybag, and a number of *rangga* poles—for example, the *djuda* (tree), *mawulan* ('walking stick', or water-producing pole), the *ganinjari* or *ganinjiri* (yam) and *djanda* (goanna; specifically, goanna tail). The dominant theme is the creative ability of the two Sisters and Brother, who have abnormal genitals. The *rangga* objects have life-giving properties, and all relate to the basic theme of fertility, expressed through the fecundity of the two women, the growth of trees and foliage, the creation of running springs and the prominent place accorded to the sun's rays. This perspective includes the procreation of man and the natural species, within the context of the rhythmic sequence of the seasons.

The Djanggawul disembarked on the mainland coast at the sacred place of Jelangbara (or Yelangbara), Port Bradshaw, and commenced their travels, in the course of which they had many adventures: eventually they disappeared westward into the setting sun. The myth and the song cycle through which it is normally conveyed are very detailed, with much symbolic allusion and meaning. As they move across the country, they use *rangga* as walking sticks, one in each hand, while conical mats containing the other *rangga* are slung over their shoulders. From time to time, they plunge one or another of these into the ground: in the case of the *mawulan*, a spring gushes forth; from the *djuda*, a tree springs up fully grown, with its parakeet-feather pendants turned into birds among the foliage. The *ngainmara* mat which holds the *rangga* is a symbolic womb: it is the source of human life, because it was from the wombs of the two Sisters that the first Aboriginal people came. The *rangga* poles are penis symbols. But they also symbolize human beings or children emerging from the wombs of the Sisters.

Two incidents from the myth are pertinent here. The first relates to this theme of birth and fertility. At Nganmarawi ('Conical Mat place'), children emerged from one of the Sisters as she opened her legs. Had she spread them too far, children would have flowed from her (as they did at other places, from both Sisters). They kept people stored in their wombs, just as *rangga* were kept in a *ngainmara*. When male children emerged, they were laid in the grass—which explains why males now have facial hair; girls were put under the *ngainmara* itself to keep them smooth and soft. The second incident occurred at Marabai. The Sisters left their sacred dillybags containing *rangga* in a bough shelter and went off to collect mangrove shells. While they were away, the Djanggawul Brother and his male companions (who had emerged from the Sisters) crept into the shelter and took the bag and its contents. The Sisters heard the cry of a *djunmal* mangrove bird, warning them that something was wrong. They hurried back, thinking their sacred bags were in danger from fire, to find their belongings gone. Men's footprints were all around, and they followed these until they heard the men singing. They stopped short, saying to each other: 'The men have taken from us, not only our songs and the emblems, but also our power to perform sacred ritual!' This power had formerly belonged only to the Sisters. But they reassured themselves: 'We know everything. We have really lost nothing ... we can let them have that small part. For aren't we still sacred, even if we have lost the bags? Haven't we still our wombs?' Aboriginal commentators (themselves men) remarked at this juncture: 'Women should really be the ritual leaders, for everything belongs to them. Men stole it all. But really we still know that they are the real leaders' (R. Berndt, *ibid.*: 40).

The *dua nara* rituals dramatize incidents in the Djanggawul's journey. Neophytes are admitted at various stages, but several years elapse before the full series is revealed. Some of these important sequences are as follows.

(a) The secret-sacred ground is prepared and a shelter constructed: *rangga* are removed from the places where they have been hidden (some in swamps), cleaned, and decorated. The shelter represents the *ngainmara* or womb, and the initiates are *rangga*. The ground itself is a projection of the womb concept. A series of preliminary songs and dances deals with the rise and fall of the surf and the sound of the sea, commemorating the voyage from Bralgu. Invocations are called to the Djanggawul, and to the sacred sites which are associated with them. (In this context and in others throughout the *nara*, women provide the participating men with food: this is, primarily, specially prepared cycad-nut 'bread', which is ritually consumed.)

(b) Actors represent various natural species connected with the Djanggawul, and novices are instructed. There is also shaving of facial hair. Older men leave on their chins small tufts which symbolize the fringe of the *ngainmara* mat (or the pubic hair of the Sisters), and attach to them orange-feathered pendants similar to those hung from *rangga* objects.

(c) In the main camp, uninitiated boys, women and girls are covered with *ngainmara* (which, although sacred, are used ordinarily): they represent the Djanggawul Sisters' children, still unborn. Men dance round them, invocations are called, and the people underneath the mats are poked—the poking represents the Djanggawul brother's penis. Also, a parallel is drawn with the Djanggawul Sisters covering newly born female infants with the *ngainmara*: when the mats are cast aside, this symbolizes birth.

(d) More dances follow, relating to natural species, and corresponding with sections of the myth. The major *rangga* are manipulated by individual actors or groups of actors, as they writhe over the ground clasping them to their bodies. They emerge from the shelter in which the objects are kept, sometimes to the accompaniment of singing or to the rhythmic beat of clapping sticks, sometimes in silence.

(e) As the men 'come down' from their ground and move toward the main camp, the women respond to their ritual cries. A leader climbs a forked post, and invocations are called while decorated women dance around him. Pairs of dancers re-enact 'totemic' dances before them. Such acts are repeated for several weeks, until men come at night bearing flaming torches. These represent the fire which the Sisters originally thought had destroyed their dillybags, only to find that they had been stolen by the men.

(f) Further dancing includes the displaying of *rangga*. Finally everyone, adults and children, bathes ritually in the sea or in a billabong. During this, invocations are called, and when the men emerge they dance various 'totemic' fish. Symbolically, this dramatizes the wetting of the *rangga* when they were brought by canoe from Bralgu: it also signifies the final hiding away of these *rangga* in a swamp or billabong. Additional meanings are also attached. Warner (*ibid.*: 353) says it represents the removal of semen. More generally, it is interpreted as an act of purification—removing ritual contagion: an act of normalization.

The Djanggawul *dua nara* is complemented by the *jiridja* (yiridja) moiety *nara*. The myth-cycle in this case is primarily the Laindjung-Banaidja. Much of it emphasizes male ritual dominance, with little direct reference to fertility, although it does concern particular natural species. It is important to bear in mind, however, that these myth cycles are not isolated but are essentially interwoven. Moreover, in the *dua* or *jiridja nara*, men and women of both moieties actively participate. It is a question of cooperation, with the interplay of managers or directors on one hand and workers on the other.

While the *dua nara* rites are more localized, they are closely associated with the western

Arnhem Land *maraiin*. In the same overall region, both in the west and in the east, is the *kunapipi* (or Gunabibi). This cult has a wide distribution. It first spread into north-eastern Arnhem Land from the Roper and Rose rivers, and there it was integrated with the local Wawalag mythology (see under ii. *Initiation*). The two Wawalag sisters are equated with the Kunapipi Mother, who in turn can manifest herself as Rainbow Snake (Yulunggul or Julunggul), in male or female form. A distinction can be drawn between the Djanggawul and the *kunapipi*. While both focus on fertility, the first emphasizes the female principle and the second the male principle. However, in any one cycle—in the Djanggawul or in the *kunapipi*—*both* elements are treated. The presence of the *kunapipi* in north-eastern Arnhem Land provides this complementary balance—but it does not necessarily do this in other areas where Kunapipi-as-Mother is emphasized. An exception, too, is the Walbiri *gadjari* (which is equivalent to the *kunapipi*). A further aspect distinguishing the *kunapipi* cult from the Djanggawul is the presence of the Wawalag, who are not regarded as creators of *human beings* (R. Berndt 1952: 10). When the *kunapipi* was introduced into north-eastern Arnhem Land, its basic ritual patterning was retained, along with the use of special sacred objects and, to some extent, their symbolic meanings (R. Berndt 1951*a*); but subincision was not accepted, although it is an integral part of *kunapipi* ritual elsewhere.

The Wawalag myth substantiates three rituals: the *djunggawon*, *kunapipi* and *ngurlmag*. The *djunggawon* re-enacts the swallowing of the two Sisters by the Python, Julunggul, and dancers represent natural species etc. which escaped from the Wawalag's cooking-fire and dived into the sacred waters of Muruwul. This section has already been discussed in relation to circumcision. The *kunapipi* covers the swallowing of young men, the presence of Julunggul after the Wawalag have been swallowed, and a number of dances relating to copulation and procreation. The *ngurlmag* focuses on the special shelter or hut of the Wawalag, involving Julunggul and other snakes. Many of these ritual sequences overlap. (See Warner *ibid.*: 290-311, in reference to the *kunapipi*.) The *ngurlmag* is not unlike the western Arnhem Land *ubar* ritual: both use the hollow drum (*uwar* or *ubar*), which symbolizes the Mother.

The *kunapipi* rituals take place on a secret-sacred ground that is triangular in shape. This stands for Julunggul's body: one side is for *dua* moiety men, the other for *jiridja*. At the apex there is a hole symbolizing Muruwul, or Miraraminar: this is the *nanggaru*, the Mother's womb. After preliminary songs and dancing in the main camp, youths are taken out to the secret-sacred ground to the accompaniment of swinging bullroarers. They are smeared with red-ochre and arm blood; women are told that they have been swallowed by the Snake. In the main camp, women crouch under *ngainmara* mats while men dance round them; this symbolizes Julunggul encircling the Wawalag in their hut. On the secret ground, men representing various natural species act out their sequences, some simulating coitus on entering the *nanggaru*: they enter this hole as the mythical creatures did when they 'ran away' from the Wawalag.

A large crescent-shaped trench (the *kanalara*) is dug on the ground and a Julunggul-image etched on its walls. Dramatic acts simulating coitus take place in this trench. Later, a large structure (12 to 20 feet high), in some cases two, is erected at its edge: this is the *jelmalandji*, and it too represents the Snake. Men dance before it, wearing conical head-dresses covered (as the *jelmalandji* is) with feather-down in a Snake design. Fire is thrown ritually (in the *djamala* section of the ritual), symbolizing lightning issuing from the

Julunggul and other mythical Snakes. Then the *jelmalandji* are pushed over and the *kanala-ra* filled in by dancing feet.

Two further ritual sequences follow. One, the exchange of wives (called the *kurangara*), is rarely carried out in Arnhem Land, but was possibly common elsewhere. Conventionally, this takes place on the *kunapipi* ground. Women, ochred and decorated with feathered headbands, dance (the *ngamamali*) before singing men who sit with heads bowed because the women are sacred—'just like the dancers in a men's secret-sacred ritual'. They use two pole emblems, one representing the Julunggul and the other a stringybark tree. Lifting the Julunggul, they hit the tree emblem, so that pieces of bark fly across the ground: this is the lightning sent by Julunggul while the Wawalag are in their hut. The women then receive presents from their male *kunapipi* partners. On the final night the *ngamamali* dances are repeated, and copulation takes place: after a man has had coitus with a woman, her husband comes to him and rubs his sweat on the man's legs and arms to prevent illness arising from this ritual act. (See R. Berndt *ibid.*: 52.)

In the other ritual sequence, the central feature is the *djepalmandji*. On a basis of two upright forked posts with a connecting horizontal pole, boughs are arranged to form a shelter. Two men climb up on to the forked posts and sit facing each other, while young novices crouch hidden under the boughs. The *djepalmandji* 'is' the hut of the Wawalag sisters. The men sitting in the forks (which are the wombs) cry ritually. Symbolically, the reference is to childbirth. Bullroarers are swung, as women and children (who are red-ochred) dance in the way the Wawalag did: they surround the *djepalmandji*, and then sit covered, to one side. Dancing men run toward the *djepalmandji* and, surrounding the shelter and the women and children, prod them with spears. The coverings are thrown aside and novices emerge from the *djepalmandji*, covered with red-ochre and blood—this is the blood of the Wawalag-as-Kunapipi. Finally, the *djepalmandji* is knocked down, and all the participants paint themselves with ochred designs representing Julunggul.

Western Arnhem Land has rituals parallel to these, but they vary considerably in detail (see R. and C. Berndt 1970: 128-42). The *ubar* (or *uwar*, in the Maung version), as noted, is primarily initiatory; but its symbolism emphasizes the Mother, who is often identified as Ngaljod, the Rainbow Snake (in male or female form). She is, however, also the Mother Waramurunggundji who, like the Djanggawul, was responsible for peopling the country—or, rather, this part of it. Spencer (1914: 270, 275-86) calls her Imberombera; Ngaljod he calls Numereji (*ibid.*: 290-305). Another important figure in the *ubar* is Yira-wadbad the Snake-man, who was referred to in relation to initiation. The *ubar* is also revelatory. In the closing sequences, the shelter on the secret-sacred ground is demolished; men dance through the flames, singeing the hairs from their legs, 'becoming like newly born people': and in the final scene the Mother 'is present' on the ground with her devotees.

While the Mother-symbolism in *ubar* aligns it with the Djanggawul, its rituals are closer to the eastern Arnhem Land *ngurlmag*, substantiated by the Wawalag mythology. Another ritual series is the *maraiin*, which is roughly equivalent in structure to the *dua* and *jiridja* moiety *nara*, but mythologically is more closely allied to the Wawalag. In ritual enactments, special shelters (representing the body of the Mother or of Ngaljod) are constructed: postulants emerge from these holding *maraiin* emblems as in the *dua nara*: invocations are called and concluding ritual bathing for all is said 'to dissipate the dangerously strong sacred aura attaching to them' (R. and C. Berndt 1970: 138).

The *kunapipi* was introduced into western Arnhem Land within the last 30-odd years, just as it was into the eastern side: the ritual sequence is similar to what has already been described, with a few variations. The Ngaljod-identification (as Snake; male or female) is, however, much more obvious. And there are ritual-song divisions. The first is the *djamala* (including the use of the *ganalara* and the *jelmalandji*), the second the *gudjiga* (including ritual coitus), and the third the *warimulunggul* (which covers all public or 'open' ritual).

Spencer (*ibid.*: 164-6, 213-8) mentions that the bullroarer is called *kunapipi* ('kunapippi') by the Djauan, Mungarai and Ngalakan, and that there is 'a very big man named Kuna-pippi'. His account is identified with the *kunapipi* discussed here, although he makes no mention of fertility. However, Spencer refers to a mythic being killing and eating a number of men and finally being killed himself: this parallels incidents in some of the *kunapipi* versions, as does the reference to women originally possessing sacred emblems which were stolen by a mythic character.

The *kunapipi* ritual, as noted, extends, over a very large region. Spreading from the Roper River area, it was brought northward into north-eastern Arnhem Land, and into the western side via the Rembranga people of south-west Arnhem Land. It also spread across the buffalo plains east of Darwin, to the Daly River and to Port Keats, and then south-west through Victoria River Downs and Wave Hill to Hooker Creek, Gordon Downs, Hall's Creek and into the southern Kimberleys of Western Australia, among other places. Kunapipi is one name for the Mother herself, but other names are also used for this ritual complex—for instance, Kalwadi (Karwadi) and Kadjari, or Gadjeri (a word which can mean 'old woman'). On Bathurst and Melville Islands there were the Earth Mothers (R. and C. Berndt 1964/68: 68-9), but without specific ritual associations, as far as we know. The Laragia and the indigenous Daly River groups built circular stone structures (as ritual grounds) which symbolized the Mother's womb.

In the sacred *kunapipi* mythology (which, of course, varies from place to place), the Mother may be a single identity, or may appear (as in the Wawalag identification) as a dual manifestation. As a projection of her, there are her daughters (sometimes two, sometimes more); in the central-west of the Northern Territory, they are called the Mungamunga. And almost everywhere this ritual-complex is found, the theme is similar. In the myth, the first people emerged from her womb: they went directly into a 'ring place' (the secret-sacred ground) for the performance of ritual. In real life, it is said that men entering their ritual ground are returning to the Mother's womb: when the rites are completed, they emerge from her womb. Berndt (1951a 144-203) discusses the source of the north-eastern Arnhem Land *kunapipi* and of the Mara and Alawa *kunapipi* song cycles. In the Mara myth, the Mungamunga entice men for copulation: when they are exhausted, Kunapipi kills and eats them whole. In some versions, she vomits their bones and, as quite often happens in myth, they are revived by ants biting them. In other cases, they are not revived. At last, Eaglehawk kills her. As she dies, her cry and the blood from her wound go into all the surrounding trees: the sound is contained in the blood. Later, Eaglehawk cuts down a tree and from a piece of its wood makes the first bullroarer, the *mumuna*. As he swings it, it 'turns into Mumuna', uttering her cry. Symbolically, the 'killing' and vomiting of the men, as in the myth, represent her true function as a creative being: that is, the admission and emission of initiated men to and from her womb.

Elkin (1961a: 166-209) describes a *yabuduruwa* ritual at Tandandjal performed by south-west Arnhem Land Aborigines (Djauan, Ngalgbun, Yangman, Mungarai and Alawa), and draws a distinction between it and the *kunapipi*. The *jabadura* (*yabuduruwa*) among the Alawa (Berndt 1951*a*: 185) is classified with the *kunapipi*, and has subincision connected with it. However, according to Elkin (*ibid.*: 167) the *kunapipi* was adopted into the *yabuduruwa* region, and the *yabuduruwa* is regarded as belonging to the *jiridja* moiety, the *kunapipi* to the *dua*. In Elkin's view (*ibid.*: 197-200), the *yabuduruwa* is allied to north-central and central Australian ritual, but also has affinities with the *jiridja* and *dua* moiety *nara* and *maraiin* of north-eastern and western Arnhem Land. (See also Maddock 1970.) Elkin's description is quite detailed. The main ingredients are a sacred shade called Nalgogo or Nagorgo (see R. and C. Berndt 1970: 122-3 regarding the mythical Nagugur father and son, responsible for introducing the *kunapipi* ritual), identified as Mummuna (*mumuna* or *mumunga*, an 'inside' name for the Kunapipi; also the sound of the bullroarer, see above; R. Berndt 1951*a*: 146-7); the hardwood gong, which parallels the *ubar* or *uwar*, and the goanna ritual (where women participate in the closing sequence), with secondary dramatic performances relating to other natural species. Elkin (174, 204) believes that these rites are concerned with 'rising from the dead', with reincarnation, and with pre-existence.

In two other articles, Elkin (1961*b*: 259-93; 1-15) describes the *maraian* (i.e., *maraiin*) at Mainoru in southern Arnhem Land. These are *dua* and *jiridja* moiety rites which, taking into account their basic terminology, are close to the *dua* and *jiridja nara* of north-eastern Arnhem Land, although they incorporate many other elements too. The parallel is not unexpected, since the *maraiin* that is traditional in the Oenpelli area has strong eastern overtones. (See R. and C. Berndt 1970: 121, 135-8; and also Spencer *ibid.*: 150-2.) Elkin's discussion (*ibid.*: 1-15) of these rituals covers their mythological context, which emphasizes an association with *muidj*—a central Arnhem Land name for Julunggul, which places this *maraiin* more closely within the framework of the *kunapipi*. However, Elkin says that the *maraiin* is not interested so much in the increase of natural species as in their spirits. As he puts it, the *maraiin* 'is primarily for the "dead", for the souls of men, and for the *maraian* or Dreaming places of the shades of natural species' (*ibid.*: 15). This differs, as we have seen, from the north-eastern Arnhem Land *dua nara* (see above) and from the western Arnhem Land *maraiin* (R. and C. Berndt *ibid.*: 135-8). But the focus on spirits is perhaps not so irrelevant in this context: they are of the Dreaming, and are considered immortal— and the power they manifest in ritual is both of a diffused and specific kind. The stress is on 'life', rather than on 'death'.

The *kunapipi* complex in the Port Keats area resembles the Mara (Roper river) version, but intermingled with additional syncretic mytho-ritual material. Stanner (1959-61: 110) speaks of Karwadi (Kalwadi) as a 'bullroarer ceremony' among the Murinbata. This word (he notes) is the secret name of 'The Mother of All', 'The Old Woman'. In the *punj* ritual, youths receive their bullroarers; the sound of these bullroarers being swung is the Mother's cry or call. In Murinbata she is called Mutjingga, the ordinary word for an 'old woman', and in the relevant myth she swallows children. She is eventually discovered by the mythic characters Left Hand and Right Hand. Right Hand kills her, slits open her belly and removes the children, who are still alive. Before she dies, she asks: '"from whom is this?" Left Hand replies "from yourself! yours was the fault!"' Stanner (*ibid.*: 260 *et seq.*) interprets this, comparing it with ritual. In his opinion it symbolizes 'a wrongful turning of life' (see especially *ibid.*: 263): 'Mutjingga is killed, but is mourned': there 'has been some kind of "immemorial misdirection" in human affairs, and ... living men are committed to its consequences'. 'The myth of the Old Woman is a story about one thing under the guise of another, and that story is thus an allegory ...' Stanner (*ibid.*: 271-2) then proceeds to give an allegorical interpretation. Whether we can accept this or not is open to question. The *karwadi* cult (he says: *ibid.*: 120) reveals 'something in the condition of human life that excites sorrow by its sad inevitability'; '... the death of the Mother is the condition of the perpetuation of human life through its children'. In another context (R. and C. Berndt 1970: 229-34), this suggestion of 'immemorial misdirection' has been referred to.

From the evidence available, it is more difficult to reconcile this with Aboriginal thinking than other explanations which can be and are put forward for the killing of the Mara Kunapipi, or for the death of Mutjingga. One can equally well see such a myth as expressing seasonal fluctuation, and a natural rhythm of birth and re-birth: and this is actually in harmony with Stanner's comment regarding the perpetuation of life through children. The myth of the Rainbow Snake (Kunmanggur) has, according to Stanner (*ibid.*: 234 *et seq.*), no ritual connotation in the Port Keats area. Without our reconstructing his arguments, he sees this mythic creature as a counterpart to the Mother, Mutjingga, as Kunmanggur 'the Father' who, through his death, enables fire to be given to man. The themes, but not necessarily Stanner's interpretations, are consistent with those in western Arnhem Land and elsewhere. Male and female attributes are seen in symbolic interaction, emphasizing the role of women in procreation, and as original owners of all power: while the Rainbow Snake (as Python, etc., with variations on that theme) is a necessary ingredient in that complementary scene.

In Stanner's case, the Snake is spoken of as 'Father'. And Warner (1937/58: 371, 384, 387) calls Yulunggul 'the Great Father Snake' (that is, Bapa Indi): but this was possibly misheard in place of the more usual expression *bapi jindi* (snake big). However, since a number of such Snakes are involved in various myths, although not all necessarily male, kin terms are often used to distinguish between them. (And in some versions of the Wawalag story, the Snake's sons, living in the waterhole with him, address him as 'father'.) In western Arnhem Land, as noted, the Rainbow Snake (Ngaljod) can be, interchangeably, the fertility Mother Waramurunggundji, or Kunapipi *or* Ngaljod. Moreover, Ngaljod can be either male or female. The Mother as Rainbow Snake (R. and C. Berndt *ibid.*: 229) has two primary manifestations, as a 'good' and as a 'bad' Mother. In her bad manifestation she is blamed for bringing disaster, or being an agent of disaster, and in some myth-versions she is 'killed' by human beings (proto-mythic). But this is not to be interpreted as a 'mythic misdirection' in Stanner's terms.

In the Port Keats situation, the separation of these two mythic concepts—the Mother, and the Rainbow Snake—is much more clear-cut, and mythic interaction between them is at a minimum.

As we move across the central west of the Northern Territory, the Kunapipi appears in her Gadjari guise. Meggitt (1966) describes this mytho-ritual constellation among the Walbiri (Wailbri). There it is known by the Aboriginal-English expression 'Big Sunday' (see R. Berndt 1951a: 14), although its correct name is *Mamandabari-maliara*: *maliara* refers to post-circumcisional or Gadjari (Gadjeri) novices, and *Mamandabari* is the name of two Dreaming characters in the myth. These two ranged over a wide stretch of country, mainly south of Hooker Creek and impinging on areas relevant to 'typically' Central Australian tribes. Their travels and the incidents which punctuate them align the myth with others of the Central and Western Desert regions, except that, as Meggitt points out, 'innovating actions performed by the heroes' are noted with little reference to 'violence, treachery, or sexual activities . .' (*ibid.*: 22). Nowhere do the Mother and the two daughters, the Mungamunga, appear, and Meggitt concludes that the northern Gadjari (or *kunapipi*) is an importation into this area: 'the indigenous Mamandabari myth provides a rationale that has a very different orientation from that underlying the Big Sunday further north' (*ibid.*: 25). However, there are some similarities in ritual paraphernalia (pits, the *nanggaru* or *ngangguru*; poles, the *gumagu* or *jelmalandji*; and firebrands, etc.) and in the song cycle itself, which has been introduced. Meggitt's study (1966), as did Berndt's (in 1951a), provides numerous examples of a common thread in *kunapipi* manifestations over a large part of the Territory. In spite of adaptation as it spreads from one area to another, basic identifying symbols are retained.

The Gadjari of the Walbiri demonstrates a nicety in balance between northern influences (expressed through the more complex *kunapipi*) and the apparent simplicity of southern (for example, Aranda) and Western Desert cult activity framed in very different terms. Meggitt (*ibid.*: 78-91) makes these comparisons: and compares the Walbiri Gadjari with the Aranda Ingkura (see Chapter Five). One common feature here is subincision. Although in the Walbiri Gadjari subincision does not take place in the course of the ritual itself, it is still a pre-requisite for senior membership (but not, as we have seen, in western and eastern Arnhem Land). In most cases, especially in northern versions, arm blood and incisure blood are identified with the Mother's blood.

Meggitt draws a distinction between the human mythic characters and/or the separation out and recognition of major or dominating beings who are inter-tribal and super-'totemic', *and* those who underline an equality of status, expressed through a 'levelling out' of southern mythic beings. These last are more obviously shape-changing and self-'totemic'. As regards the first, this is not invariably so in the mythology of the north. Certainly it applies to some extent to the Kunapipi and those with whom she is identified: but the great mobile myths do accommodate to local belief systems, and recognize also a large number of 'secondary' beings. The problem is complex, and broad distinctions or contrasts of this kind are not really satisfactory. It is true that certain northern beings appear to be singled out or to have achieved mythic or ritual prominence: but a lot depends on their ritual circumstance and on the structural form this can take. One thing that is significant in this context is ritual ownership. In southern Desert regions, and among the Walbiri (and Aranda), this is much more sharply defined in relation to the local descent group or its equivalent. In the north, although the local descent group is basically significant, ownership is more widely diffused. The problem of 'totemic' expression is even more difficult. Many of the great northern mythic beings assume responsibility for the emergence, creation, or designation of natural species and other aspects of the natural environment, while not themselves being 'totemic'. Yet there are exceptions to that rule. However, southern mythic beings are much more directly both— both human *and* animal etc., simultaneously. Meggitt (*ibid.*: 83) believes this is because of 'individual possession of conception totems' in the north. It is possible that in the north, as far as a person's spirit is concerned, the 'totem' serves as an intermediary or agent, while in the south it is more directly myth-

linked. Taking into account differences between the north and the south, broadly interpreted, it is suggested that the Walbiri have devalued 'the elements of sexuality and human
fertility, and they have re-interpreted [these] ... to fit in with their ethos of male pre-
dominance' (*ibid.*: 84). In the north, as we have seen, both male and female aspects are
treated, although female fertility is often more obvious.

Although the *kunapipi* did not flourish as an active cult in its own right among the
Walbiri, and was subordinated to local emphases, in the nearby Wave Hill area and
westward (including Birrundudu) it was significant under the name Gadjari. In R. and C.
Berndt (1946: 72, 75; 1950: 185-88, with plates), drawings depict the Gadjari, in either solo
or dual form (as the Mungamunga), from whose womb postulants flow into a ring place for
secret-sacred activity. Present-day initiates entering this ground are said to be entering the
Mother, or Old Woman. There is also the ritual throwing of fire, the use of bullroarers, and
the erection of the tall *gumagu* structure. This last can be worn as a headdress, as among the
Walbiri, or men can mount on one another's shoulders to form a symbolic *gumagu*, as among
the Njining. The *gumagu* itself has meandering designs in feather-down and ochre on a basis
of brush and bark, and represents the Mother. In some instances she wears a pearlshell
pubic covering suspended from a human hair waistband, along with a headband and
nosebone, and sometimes she has pearlshell eyes. The design has also been said to represent
the Rainbow Snake upon the Mother. This structure is erected like the Arnhem Land
jelmalandji.

Within this broad region are the women's secret rituals of *djarada* and *jawalju*, which are
roughly comparable to the male Gadjari, but with at least one major difference—namely,
men do not participate in them, although women do have a part to play in the Gadjari.
The *djarada* and *jawalju* have some elements in common (C. Berndt 1950a: 28): their
material equipment includes a long stick or spear, a phallic symbol, and both contain love
magic elements. The *djarada* (*ibid.*: 30-42) is the northern variety which had its genesis in
the *kunapipi*. The guardian spirits are the Mungamunga girls, two or more, said to be
associated with rain and with the Rainbow Snake: they provide the power and the sanction
for *djarada* performances. Among other linkages with the *kunapipi* are the possum dancing,
which resembles that carried out by men, and the chickenhawk dancing. Further,
women's dancing should take place in a special 'ring-place'. The *jawalju* (*ibid.*: 43-51) is
mainly associated with southern traditions, for example Walbiri and Waneiga; one spirit
character held responsible for this ritual is Ininguru (Ini-nguru), frequently translated as
Whirlwind. An alternative name is Yuguruguru, said to be a Waneiga name for two spirit
women, equivalent to the Mungamunga and called by the Walbiri Yabadjaudjau and
Urunganada, sometimes regarded as two female spirit beings. The impreciseness of mythic
identification suggests a combination of introduced Gadjari-Mungamunga elements and
local ones—as in the Gadjari discussed by Meggitt. Here too there are linkages with male
ritual and mythology, although it is more correct to speak of men and women holding in
common a body of mythology from which they select certain segments for their own particular use. For example, the name *jawalju* itself refers to a large black goanna; the Rainbow
Snake is noted, as well as the *djundagal* snake which more usually appears in other myth-
ritual complexes. And *jawalju* dancing includes re-enactment of the travels and activities
of such beings. (See also C. Berndt 1965: 241-73, who discusses this comparatively on a
wider frame, and the earlier work of Kaberry 1939: 255-68, and Róheim 1933.)

In the eastern and southern Kimberleys, extending to the Balgo area, an adult man is involved in his cult 'lodge' rituals after subincision—either specifically in relation to them or, more generally, participating with others in the dramatizing of the great mythic cycles, sections of which belong to members of particular local descent groups. Among their sacred objects and emblems are wooden boards that are regarded as 'set apart' or tabu (*darugu*). The mythic characters are very numerous, but principally they include the Ganabuda (equivalent to the Gadjari, the Mother: but sometimes identified with a group of women, sometimes with their male counterparts), and a range of others typical of Desert mythology. For example, there are the Wadi Gudara, Two Men (parallelling Meggitt's Mamandabari), Malu the Kangaroo man, and so on. The Ganabuda appear in two main traditions. Petri (1968) mentions similar traditions among people living in the neighbourhood of Anna Plains and La Grange. In the Balgo region, they are associated with the *kunapipi*: one tradition comes from the Walbiri-Waneiga to the east, the other from the Djaru to the north-east. Considerable admixture of these has resulted in a situation not unlike that discussed by Meggitt for the Walbiri. In other words, the Gadjari in its ritual manifestation, but not necessarily in its mythology, has spread extensively over the Desert—to Jigalong on the south-west, and south in the direction of the Warburtons.

The primary ritual expressions are the *dingari* and the *gurangara*. The *gurangara* is especially interesting since it bears the same name as the *kurangara* (*gurangara*) section of the *kunapipi*—although that, as already mentioned, includes ritual sex relations between persons who in ordinary life would be tabu to each other in this respect. (See R. Berndt 1951*a*: 48, 52).

Piddington (1932: 81-2) mentions the *gurangara* for the Karadjeri, but mainly as a rite in which sacred objects are revealed to subincised youths. Lommel (1952: 82-8) also discusses it, and so do Petri (1950*a*: 43-51; 1954: 243; 1967; 1968: 189, 190) and Worms (1942: 208-35). Lommel (1950: 21-4) treats it as a new cult from the perspective of the Unambal, and as having come from the south, whereas among the nearby Ungarinyin it had been fully developed. Mythic substantiation is not clear, but one presiding being is Djanba, the son of Nguniai. Sacred posts or slabs are revealed to initiates, and there are ritual feasts. Lommel's interpretation of this was criticized (R. Berndt 1951*b*: 229-35), mainly on the score of his assertion that it was a 'cult of despair'. However, the Unambal cult showed many aspects of alien influence. It is true that, with the spread of a cult of this kind, there is often an amalgamation or accretion or modification of elements which are re-structured to suit the local religious situation, even though this is by no means a one-way process. In the Gadjari of the Walbiri many of the northern features do not appear, and to some extent this is the case for the southern Kimberleys. Nevertheless, basic elements can still be identified and are recognized as such. The *gurangara* in some areas is considered to be part of the Gadjari, and in the central west of the Northern Territory is also known as the *wilbibi*. In that form it is associated with the mythic being Djanba who, in turn, is linked to the Gadjari. Meggitt (1966: 87) speaks of the *gurangara* as forming 'a quite different kind of cult in conjunction with the Djanba', and says it came into the Kimberleys from the south. There are several problems here which will not be discussed (but see Meggitt 1955; Worms 1950, 1952; Petri 1956, 1968: 253-55).

Returning to the Balgo area (where the main 'tribes' are Walmadjeri, Gugadja-Mandjil-djara, and some Ngadi or Ngari), the two major rituals, as noted, are the *dingari* (see also

Petri 1968: 306, 307, 309) and *gurangara*. Broadly speaking, and taking into account the admixture of southern and northern elements, both belong to the Gadjari complex. The Ganabuda are equivalent to the Gadjari. The name refers to a group of mythic women possessed of magical powers who originally, in the Dreaming, had ritual knowledge denied to men. They travelled either alone or with a *dingari* ritual group who were also the food-collectors. They are associated also with other 'totemic' beings. Finally, their power was taken over by the men. In these myths, too, 'totemic' leaders revealed to novices or postulants the secret-sacred *darugu* boards; they performed rites, including initiation; and they treated the powerful *darugu*, in the course of their ordinary travels, as objects of direct utility: for instance, as vehicles on which to fly through the sky. *Darugu* can still, men say, serve that same purpose, as well as playing their usual role in the more conventional ritual context. In the mythical scene they were also weapons and tools, for hunting game, or making waterholes or soaks or shaping the physiographic features of the countryside in much the same way as the Djanggawul manipulated their *rangga* (see above). The *dingari* rituals are essentially re-enactments of these mythic incidents. Bullroarers are swung and there are 'totemic' dances and decorated *darugu* boards. The *nanggaru* pit is commonly in use; novices sit in this while firebrands are thrown over them. Some ritual acts are performed in the *ganala* trench: novices are ritually smoked, and the *dingari* ground symbolizes the Mother—men enter and leave her womb. In the *dingari*, as in the *gurangara*, women are responsible for complementary rites held in the main camp or near the secret-sacred ground—such as the *bandiri* (or *bandimi*) dancing, which is widely performed under the same or different names (e.g. in the Wave Hill-Birrundudu area). They not only attend the *gurangara* but also participate in sections of the men's ritual. One of the most important features is the *mididi*, or *midajidi*, feast (noted by Piddington 1932: 65 and Petri 1960b). This feast is prepared by women who stand in defined relationships to postulants and novices, and it takes place at the time the *darugu* are explained to the youths (see R. Berndt 1970c).

In general, these rituals are oriented toward the maintenance of a state of affairs first instituted by the mythic beings. They are a means of direct contact with those beings, to ensure that their power is brought to bear on social living. It is believed to do this in two interrrelated ways. One emphasizes natural increase and fructification of the countryside, thus maintaining and sustaining the material things of life. The other emphasizes spiritual renewal and stimulation of the human beings involved. (See R. Berndt, *ibid.*: 216-47).

ADDITIONAL SOURCES

Throughout the regions considered here, there are a number of other rituals, but within the limitations set by this volume it is not possible to discuss them all. For the most part, only dominant trends have been mentioned. The *Wanderkulte* are a case in point. These have been discussed by Lommel (1952: 77-90) and Petri (1968: 143, 157, 236; 1970). Many of them are in fact linked with the great cult-cycles, or subsumed by those cycles; others are very similar to some of the Desert 'meandering' mytho-ritual constellations. The Wondjina (Wandjina) cult of the Kimberleys, with its outstanding cave-paintings, has been discussed by several writers (for example, by Elkin, 1930; 1948; 1964, Petri 1954; Worms 1955, and Crawford 1968). The Wondjina are mythic beings, both male and female, who are creators and guardians. Some are related to the Rainbow Snake, Ungud: for example, Wondjina spirits come forth from the eggs of Ungud and transform themselves as Ungud. From the evidence available, it would seem that parallels can be drawn with the Ngaljod-Julunggul manifestations of western and northeastern Arnhem Land. Hernández (1961: 115-9) discusses the 'Galoru' (or Kaleru) as well as the Ungud (which he calls Ungur), each belonging to a different moiety and each associated with spirit children. Speaking of the Drysdale River people, Hernández (*ibid.*: 122-3) says that the *mayangari* ceremony (derived from *mayange*, bullroarer) essentially commemorates 'the principal things of creation' and that these are associated with Ungud and Galoru. In addition to these references, see Love (1935), Worms (1940; 1942), Petri (1950*b*), Elkin (1933) and Kaberry (1939).

THE ICONOGRAPHIC CONTEXT

In this regional span, the two 'open ends' of the life-cycle continuum are marked by a relative lack of ritual objects, although as far as death is concerned there is an exception. As regards birth, the mythic linkage between the spirit which emerges from the Dreaming and its human container is sufficient without visible concomitant symbols. It is true that a pregnant woman in western Arnhem Land carried a small dillybag in which the spirit of the child resided for a while; that in many areas 'totemic' or local group wells or watering places were associated with such spirits; and that in the Kimberleys a Wondjina head was re-touched in order to ensure the supply of spirit children. But in general, birth requires no specific ritual extension or symbolism. It is in itself a rite, and serves as a basis for the symbolism of initiation and of an appreciable amount of secret-sacred ritual, in one way or another.

Northern mortuary rituals provide a colourful example of the dominance of material representations. This is in marked contrast to what happens elsewhere, where emblemic designs and objects are hardly relevant at all. The reasons for this difference are uncertain. It is likely that it is associated, in the north, with a greater focus on the overt aspects of the sacred in the task of removing the deceased's spirit from the human life cycle. And this is a much more onerous business than, for example, among the Walbiri. Or to put it another way, in the north, death is itself a sacred rite in which the deceased is a participant; farther south, removal of the deceased's spirit into the Dreaming requires no specific impetus—it flows more naturally, as in the case of birth.

On the north coast of Arnhem Land, tall decorated hollow logs are used as receptacles for the deceased's bones, on the assumption that they are equivalent to *rangga* emblems, and are consequently returned to their 'totemic' home or to their rightful womb. Variations on this theme are obvious, when one considers that the logs themselves are often shaped to represent 'totemic' creatures, and are decorated with designs relevant to the deceased's sacred clan patterning derived from the country in which he originated. The ritual-symbolic paraphernalia of mortuary ritual are extensive: not only tall logs, but masts and flags, and sculptured *wuramu* figures of Indonesian influence. These are memorial posts, some in the stylized image of the deceased. North-eastern Arnhem Land death rituals are perhaps the most spectacular of all in Aboriginal Australia, especially in relation to their dancing and singing. In western Arnhem Land, and on Groote Eylandt, mortuary rites are closely associated with secret-sacred dancing; in the former, men are decorated as in the *maraiin*; in the latter, sacred objects are used in totemic dancing. Bathurst and Melville Islanders produce their elaborate burial posts and perform a wide range of totemic dances: but these are not as extensive as in eastern Arnhem Land, and the posts themselves are functionally different. It has been said (Mountford 1958: 60-121) that the shape of the posts and the designs painted on them are not associated with myth: some are, however, representations of human beings. For the rest of the region under discussion, death and burial are relatively simple acts in so far as the use of objects is concerned.

Initiation involves a wide range of ritual objects, but designs and symbolic associations are predominantly expressed through the decoration of actors in specific 'totemic' and other performances. Basically, the bullroarer is a sign of initiation, although it is not used in north-eastern or western Arnhem Land, nor on Bathurst and Melville Islands. It entered Arnhem Land through the *kunapipi*, and is more generally associated with both circumcision *and* subincision. In north-eastern Arnhem Land circumcision is the rule, but in western Arnhem Land it is non-traditional and still rare, and on Bathurst and Melville Islands it is absent. The bullroarer in its circumcisional aspect represents both the Mother *and* the penis, and this is clear too in the *kalwadi* of the Murinbata, as it is among the Walbiri. One variety of the Walbiri bullroarer is a small *windilburu* which has incised upon it the markings of a youth's conception Dreaming. The symbolism of the bullroarer is complex. It is treated as a living thing, and is anointed with red-ochre and blood. When swung, its cry is the voice of the Mother or some other mythic being; when held ritually, it is usually an erect penis; when given to a youth at the conclusion of his initiation, or of one phase of his initiation, it represents part of himself. In brief, the bullroarer is a symbol of life.

In Arnhem Land, initiation rites are part of the great religious cults, and the symbolism hinges on fertility. The material equipment includes *wangidja* posts representing the Wawalag Sisters; the *julunggul* (Python) trumpet and *ngainmara* mats in the east; and, in the west, the *ubar* (Mother/Ngaljod) drum, and the forked stick from which the *lida* rattle is swung and invocations called. In the north, a novice is subordinated to the overall ritual procedure which dominates the scene. In the south, as well as at Port Keats, the emphasis is on doing something for the novice, on bringing him into the orbit of the sacred. In both cases, of course, the intention is to introduce novices to the secret-sacred; but, given this, the orientations remain substantially different. In the *kulama*, too, the novice is subordinated to other, ritual, interests. In that case, this has led to the development of elaborate body decorations along with the use of a range of virtually archaic objects—goose-feather balls, bark armlets, cane arm-rings, ornate bark baskets and ceremonial belts—some of which are also used in mortuary ritual.

In contrast to the northern pattern, the Walbiri, along with tribes to the west and south-west of Wave Hill, including the Kimberleys and part of the Western Desert, combine the bullroarer with the long incised secret-sacred wooden boards. These boards belong more to the primary religious expressions than to initiation *per se*. The Walbiri show them to their novices after circumcision; in the Balgo area, the showing takes place after subincision. There are also the sacred slab posts of the northern Kimberleys (Unambal), which are a combination of the Desert-type board and the north-eastern Arnhem Land *rangga*. A further object which is not found in northern areas is the *wanigi*. In its simplest form this is a string-cross, which really belongs to the Desert tradition. One of the Walbiri examples is constructed on the basis of *jarandalba* boards.

The 'Fertility Cults' provide most iconographic examples. Two features need to be kept in mind. One is the decoration of participants and the emblems they wear: these must be seen in relation to any ritual and as part of the total representation. The other relates to the difference between northern and southern (or north-central and north-western) body decorations in the most important ritual sequences. In the north, bodies are painted in ochred designs; the only major exception to this is the *kunapipi*, where feather-down or a substitute (wild cotton) is applied to the body with blood to form typical patterns. For most other areas, in secret-sacred ritual the preference is for feather-down decorations. In women's rituals such as the *djarada* and *jawalju*, however, ochre (and charcoal etc.) is virtually always used in the patterning of body-designs.

The *dua* moiety Djanggawul is distinguished by the *rangga* poles, the *djuda, mawulan, djanda* and *ganinjiri*,which are believed to have life-producing properties, in conjunction with special dillybags and the *ngainmara* mats. The *jiridja* moiety rituals employ other *rangga*, along with the *banaidja* barramundi fish in the shape of a bound paperbark pad which is ritually beaten on the ground: this is one manifestation of Laindjung. These are complemented by the western Arnhem Land *maraiin*, the setting for a wide range of realistic and stylized representations of natural species and other phenomena. In the *kunapipi*, the actual ground shape receives major consideration, especially in regard to the *nanggaru* and *kanalara*. The great *jelmalandji* (as Rainbow Snake/Python/Mother) dominates the scene in the north, as it does in the Gadjari, where it is called *gumagu*. There is the forked *djebalmandji*, which appears in other ritual contexts as a single post from which invocations are called. The hollow log-drum (*ubar*) is paralleled by a hardwood gong in the Yabuduruwa.

A clue to the difference in religious focus, when comparing northern with central Australian or Desert manifestations, rests, not so much in the fact that different physical environments are involved, but rather in divergent attitudes toward women and the differing roles of the sexes in the scheme of social life. In the north, ritual emphasis fluctuates between a predominating focus on the female as creator and stimulator of all ritual life, and an attempt to view her position in balance with that of the male: and this is sometimes expressed through male forces which are seen as being antithetical to females. In the Desert and in Central Australia, the stress is much more directly on male generative attributes, with feminine elements subordinated and women playing a more sharply defined submissive role on socio-ritual occasions. Of course, such contrasts are broadly drawn, and empirical details relevant to any one particular region are not necessarily as clear-cut as all this. However, it is without question that in the north the physiological functions, of the female mainly but also of the male, are much more obviously brought out in ritual and in mythology. In the Desert, the mythic role of the sexes is reversed. In the north, too, as in northeastern and western Arnhem Land (as prime examples) and in other areas where the fertility cults have spread—including the northern-Desert border area of Balgo in the southern Kimberleys, but excluding Bathurst and Melville Islands on one hand and Hooker's Creek (at least as far as the southern Walbiri are concerned) on the other hand—mythic accounts specifically have it that women originally possessed all sacred rites and emblems. Only through trickery or through some form of persuasion, were men able to gain the keys to ritual life: or, it could be said, a key to the sacred and to spiritual renewal. Women, according to this view, are *naturally* sacred because of their innate creative ability. It is this element which, in one form or another, appears in much of the northern mythology and is reflected in ritual action. It is a symbolic discourse between the sexes, reinforcing their separate but complementary roles and responsibilities in significant and crucial areas of social living. Nevertheless, while accepting this, it is undeniable that men have the principal executive role in religious activity, and that they have this throughout the greater part of Aboriginal Australia. But to emphasize this alone is to ignore the complexity of the situation and to undervalue the importance of the relations between the sexes in this respect. In many areas, although not all, women have their own religious ritual which mirrors or reflects basic male-dominated ritual and in some cases closely parallels it. It could perhaps be said that women's ritual is not a reflection of the men's, that in fact the opposite is true: that male ritual is really an elaboration of women's ritual. This would be taking the matter too far, and would be just as distorted as the old view that Aboriginal women had little or no part to play in male ritual.

Religious ritual concerns all persons, of both sexes and all ages, and the fact that some persons have different spheres of participation does not invalidate that proposition. No important ritual cycle can be set in motion without the active support of the majority of persons of both sexes; and economic cooperation, important as this is, comprises only one aspect of the total picture. Equally important is the *actual* participation of women in the great cycles, either in the main camp or elsewhere (and in rare instances actually on the men's secret-sacred ground), tacitly supporting, sometimes dancing or singing or observing some conventional attitude or restriction *vis-à-vis* the ongoing ritual. This is by no means a negative or passive support—not as far as traditional Aboriginal situations are or were concerned. Involvement in religious matters, in varying degrees, by all members of a community is (or was) seen as a crucial commitment.

One interesting feature of the fertility cults is their propensity to move (i.e., be conveyed and transmitted) into and through many very different tribal areas, while retaining in the process basic elements which enable us to identify them in spite of their adaptability and flexibility in particular circumstances. In one sense, we can speak of fertility cult 'density' in the Arnhem Land-Daly River-Port Keats region, although there are local exceptions. In these areas, specific cultural expressions of this kind appear to have been indigenous and the incoming *kunapipi* (for example) simply reinforced what was already there. At the same time, that provided a stimulus to the *kunapipi* itself, of sufficient impetus to enable it to extend over a very wide area indeed—incorporating, as it did so, much of what was already mytho-ritually significant, again in local and indigenous terms. So that the *kunapipi* presents many different faces, all expressing a basic intent. In the southern Kimberleys, however, the *dingari* manifestations are not so clearly identified with the *kunapipi*, not in northern terms. There we are on the fringe of a different emphasis, and this point is brought out by Meggitt in his analysis of the Mamandabari Gadjari complex.

BIBLIOGRAPHY

Basedow, H. 1907. Anthropological Notes on the Western Coastal Tribes of the Northern Territory of South Australia, *Transactions of the Royal Society of South Australia*, Vol. XXXI.
Berndt, C. H. 1950a. *Women's Changing Ceremonies in Northern Australia*: L'Homme, I, Hermann, Paris.

Berndt, C. H. 1950b. Expressions of Grief among Aboriginal Women, *Oceania*, Vol. XX, No. 4.
Berndt, C. H. 1965. Women and the "Secret Life". In *Aboriginal Man in Australia* (R. M. and C. H. Berndt, eds.).
Berndt, C. H. 1970. Monsoon and Honey Wind. In *Échanges et Communications*, mélanges offerts à Claude Lévi-Strauss (J. Pouillon et P. Maranda, eds.): Mouton, La Hague.
Berndt, R. M. 1948a. Badu, Islands of the Spirits, *Oceania*, Vol. XIX, No. 2.
Berndt, R. M. 1948b. A Wonguri-Mandjikai Song Cycle of the Moon-Bone, *Oceania*, Vol. XIX, No. 1.
Berndt, R. M. 1951a. *Kunapipi*. A study of an Australian Aboriginal Religious Cult: Cheshire, Melbourne.
Berndt, R. M. 1951b. Influence of European Contact on Australian Aborigines, *Oceania*, Vol. XXI, No. 3.
Berndt, R. M. 1952. *Djanggawul*. An Aboriginal religious cult of north-eastern Arnhem Land: Cheshire, Melbourne (Routledge and Kegan Paul, London).
Berndt, R. M. 1952a. Subincision in a Non-Subincising Area, *American Imago*, Vol. 8, No. 2.
Berndt, R. M. 1952b. Circumcision in a Non-Circumcising Area, *International Archives of Ethnology*, Vol. XLVI, No. 2.
Berndt, R. M. 1965. Law and Order in Aboriginal Australia. In *Aboriginal Man in Australia* (R. M. and C. H. Berndt, eds.).
Berndt, R. M. 1966. Dominant Social Relationships among the Gunwinggu and 'Murngin' of Aboriginal Australia: Wenner-Gren Foundation for Anthropological Research, Burg Wartenstein. Part 2, No. 9. In *Kinship and Culture* (F. L. K. Hsu, ed.): 1971 Aldine Publishing Company, Chicago.
Berndt, R. M. ed. 1970a. *Australian Aboriginal Anthropology*: University of Western Australia Press, Perth.
Berndt, R. M. 1970b. Two in One, and More in Two. In *Échanges et Communications*, mélanges offerts à Claude Lévi-Strauss (J. Pouillon et P. Maranda, eds.): Mouton, La Hague.
Berndt, R. M. 1970c. Traditional Morality as Expressed through the medium of an Australian Aboriginal Religion. In *Australian Aboriginal Anthropology* (R. M. Berndt, ed.).
Berndt, R. M. 1972. The Walmadjeri-Gugadja. In *Hunters and Gatherers Today* (M. G. Bicchieri, ed.): Holt, Rinehart and Winston, New York.
Berndt, R. M. and C. H. Berndt. 1946. The Eternal Ones of the Dream, *Oceania*, Vol. XVII, No. 1.
Berndt, R. M. and C. H. Berndt. 1950. Aboriginal Art in Central Western Northern Territory, *Meanjin*, Vol. 9. No. 3.
Berndt, R. M. and C. H. Berndt. 1951. *Sexual Behaviour in Western Arnhem Land*: Viking Fund Publications in Anthropology, No. 16, New York.
Berndt, R. M. and C. H. Berndt. 1964/68. *The World of the First Australians*: Ure Smith, Sydney.
Berndt, R. M. and C. H. Berndt, eds. 1965. *Aboriginal Man in Australia*: Angus and Robertson, Sydney.
Berndt, R. M. and C. H. Berndt. 1970. *Man, Land and Myth in North Australia*: the Gunwinggu people: Ure Smith, Sydney.
Brandl, M. 1970. Adaptation or Disintegration? Changes in the Kulama Initiation and Increase Ritual of Melville and Bathurst Islands, Northern Territory of Australia, *Anthropological Forum*, Vol. II, No. 4.
Brandl, M. 1971. Pukumani: the social context of bereavement in a North Australian Aboriginal Tribe. Ph. D. thesis, Department of Anthropology, University of Western Australia.
Craig, B. F. (Compiler). 1966. *Arnhem Land Peninsular Region* (including Bathurst and Melville Islands): Bibliography Series, No. 1; Occasional Papers in Aboriginal Studies, No. 8, Australian Institute of Aboriginal Studies, Canberra.
Craig, B. F. (Compiler). 1968. *Kimberley Region: an Annotated Bibliography*: Bibliography Series, No. 3; Australian Aboriginal Series, No. 13, Australian Institute of Aboriginal Studies, Canberra.
Crawford, I. M. 1968. *The Art of the Wandjina*: Oxford University Press, Melbourne.
Elkin, A. P. 1930. Rock Paintings of North-West Australia, *Oceania*, Vol. I, No. 3.
Elkin, A. P. 1933. *Studies in Australian Totemism*: Oceania Monographs, No. 2, Australian National Research Council, Sydney.
Elkin, A. P. 1936. Initiation in the Bard Tribe, North-West Australia, *Journal and Proceedings of the Royal Society of New South Wales*, Vol. LXIX.
Elkin, A. P. 1938/64. *The Australian Aborigines*: Angus and Robertson, Sydney.
Elkin, A. P. 1948. Grey's Northern Kimberley Cave-Paintings Re-found, *Oceania*, Vol. XIX, No. 1.
Elkin, A. P. 1961a. The Yabuduruwa, *Oceania*, Vol. XXXI, No. 3.
Elkin, A. P. 1961b. Maraian at Mainoru, 1949, *Oceania*, Vol. XXXI, No. 4; Vol. XXXII, No. 1.
Falkenberg, J. 1962. *Kin and Totem*: Humanities Press, New York.

Goodale, J. C. 1959a. The Tiwi Dance for the Dead, *Expedition*, Bulletin of the University of Pennsylvania, Vol. 2, No. 1.

Goodale, J. C. 1959b. The Tiwi Women of Melville Island, North Australia. Ph. D. thesis in Anthropology, University of Pennsylvania.

Goodale, J. C. 1970. An example of ritual change among the Tiwi of Melville Island. In *Diprotodon to Detribalization* (A. R. Pilling and R. A. Waterman, eds.): Michigan State University Press, East Lansing.

Goodale, J. C. 1971. *Tiwi Wives*: a study of women of Melville Island, North Australia: University of Washington Press, Seattle.

Hart, C. W. M. and A. R. Pilling. 1960. *The Tiwi of North Australia*: Holt, New York.

Hernández, T. 1961. Myths and Symbols of the Drysdale River Aborigines, *Oceania*, Vol. XXXII, No. 2.

Kaberry, P. M. 1935. Death and deferred Mourning Ceremonies in the Forrest River Tribes, North-West Australia, *Oceania*, Vol. VI, No. 1.

Kaberry, P. M. 1936. Spirit-Children and Spirit-Centres of the North Kimberley Division, West Australia, *Oceania*, Vol. VI, No. 4.

Kaberry, P. M. 1939. *Aboriginal Woman*, Sacred and Profane: Routledge, London.

Lévi-Strauss, C. 1962. *La Pensée sauvage*: Plon, Paris.

Lommel, A. 1949. Notes on Sexual Behaviour and Initiation, Wunambal Tribe, North-Western Australia, *Oceania*, Vol. XX, No. 2.

Lommel, A. 1950. Modern Culture Influences on the Aborigines, *Oceania*, Vol. XXI, No. 1.

Lommel, A. 1952. *Die Unambal, ein Stamm in Nordwest-Australien*: im Selbstverlag des Museums für Völkerkunde, Hamburg.

Love, J. R. B. 1935. Mythology, Totemism and Religion of the Worora Tribe of North-West Australia, *Report of the Australian and New Zealand Association for the Advancement of Science*, Vol. XXII.

Maddock, K. 1970. Imagery and Social Structure at Two Dalabon Rock Art Sites, *Anthropological Forum*, Vol. II, No. 4.

Meggitt, M. J. 1955. Djanba among the Walbiri, Central Australia, *Anthropos*, Vol. 50.

Meggitt, M. J. 1962. *Desert People*: Angus and Robertson, Sydney.

Meggitt, M. J. 1966. *Gadjari among the Walbiri Aborigines of Central Australia*: Oceania Monographs, No. 14, University of Sydney, Sydney.

Montagu, Ashley- M. F. 1937. *Coming into Being Among the Australian Aborigines*: Routledge, London.

Mountford, C. P. 1958. *The Tiwi*: their Art, Myth and Ceremony: Phoenix House, London (Georgian House, Melbourne).

Munn, N. 1970. The Transformation of Subjects into Objects in Walbiri and Pitjantjatjara Myth. In *Australian Aboriginal Anthropology* (R. M. Berndt, ed.).

Petri, H. 1950a. Kuràngara. Neue magische Kulte in Nordwest-Australien, *Zeitschrift für Ethnologie* Band 75.

Petri, H. 1950b. Wandlungen in der geistigen Kultur nordwestaustralischer Stämme, *Veröffentlichungen aus dem Museum für Natur-Völker-und Handelskunde in Bremen*, Reihe B, Heft 1.

Petri, H. 1954. *Sterbende Welt in Nordwestaustralien*: A. Limbach, Braunschweig.

Petri, H. 1956. Dynamik im Stammesleben Nordwest-Australiens, *Paideuma*, Bd. VI/3.

Petri, H. 1960a. Alterklassen der Vorinitiation bei Eingeborenen-Gruppen Nordwestaustraliens, *Ethnologica*, N.F. Bd. 2, S.

Petri, H. 1960b. Summary of a talk entitled 'Anthropological research in the Kimberley Area of Western Australia', Anthropological Society of Western Australia: mimeographed.

Petri, H. 1967. 'Wandji-kurang-gara', ein mythischer Traditionskomplex aus der Westlichen Wüste Australiens, *Baetsler Archiv*, N.F. Bd. XV.

Petri, H. 1968. Australische Eingeborenen-Religionen (Worms-Petri). In *Die Religionen der Südsee und Australiens* (H. Nevermann, E. A. Worms and H. Petri): W. Kohlhammer, Verlag, Stuttgart.

Petri, H. and G. Petri-Odermann, 1970. Stability and Change: Present-day Historic Aspects Among Australian Aborigines. In *Australian Aboriginal Anthropology* (R. M. Berndt, ed.).

Piddington, R. 1932. Karadjeri Initiation, *Oceania*, Vol. III, No. 1

Radcliffe-Brown, A. R. *et al.* 1931. The Rainbow-Serpent Myth in South-East Australia, *Oceania*, Vol. 1, No. 3.

Róheim, G. 1933. Women and their life in Central Australia, *Journal of the Royal Anthropological Institute*, Vol. LXIII.

Spencer, B. 1914. *Native Tribes of the Northern Territory of Australia*: Macmillan, London.

Stanner, W. E. H. 1933. The Daly River Tribes. A Report of Fieldwork in North Australia, *Oceania*, Vol. IV, No. 1.

Stanner, W. E. H. 1936. Murinbata Kinship and Totemism, *Oceania*, Vol. VII, No. 2.

Stanner, W. E. H. 1959-61. On Aboriginal Religion, *Oceania*, Vol. XXX, Nos. 2 and 4; Vol. XXXI, Nos. 2 and 4; Vol. XXXII, No. 2.

Turner, D. 1970. The Wanungamagaljuagba and their neighbours: a study in adaptation. Ph. D. thesis, Department of Anthropology, University of Western Australia.

Warner, W. L. 1937/58. *A Black Civilization*: Harper, New York and London.

Worms, E. A. 1938. Die Initiationsfeiern einiger Küsten- und Binnenlandstämme in Nord-West Australien, *Annali Lateranensi*, Vol. 11.

Worms, E. A. 1940. Religiöse Vorstellungen und Kultur einiger Nord-Westaustralischen Stämme in fünfzig Legenden, *Annali Lateranenci*, Vol. 14.

Worms, E. A. 1942. Die Goranara-Feier im Australischen Kimberley, *Annali Lateranensi*, Vol. VI.

Worms, E. A. 1950. Djamar, the Creator, *Anthropos*, Bd. 45.

Worms, E. A. 1952. Djamar and his Relations to other Culture Heroes, *Anthropos*, Bd. 47.

Worms, E. A. 1955. Contemporary and Prehistoric Rock Paintings in Central and Northern Kimberley, *Anthropos*, Bd. 50.

ILLUSTRATIONS

PREAMBLE

This Fascicle comprises one Chapter, relating to North Australia. The region is very extensive indeed, and a wide range of illustrations is available for it. None, however, represent the important Port Keats-Daly River areas. I have been unable to obtain any from outside sources; my own series were damaged during the wet season floods there in 1945-46: additionally, fear of sorcery made photography extremely difficult at that time. As regards the Wailbri (Walbiri) and tribes living in the Wave Hill-Birrundudu-Balgo (southern Kimberleys) region, photographs relevant to their religious life appear in Fascicle Four since they represent 'transitional areas'.

The illustrations in this Fascicle relate mainly to the great Fertility cults, although a selection is included from the northern Kimberleys.

ACKNOWLEDGEMENTS

Figures 4, 14, 19-20, 24-25 come from the Rev. H. Shepherdson, who kindly supplied R. Berndt with a large series of photographs taken at Milingimbi in the late 1930's, before he established the mission station at Elcho Island: see R. Berndt, *An Adjustment Movement in Arnhem Land*, Paris, 1962. Figures 29-32 have been provided by Mr. C. P. Mountford of the South Australian Museum, and Figures 33-36 by Dr. Ian M. Crawford of the Western Australian Museum. Figures 37-43 are from Mr. Bruce Shaw, postgraduate research student in the Department of Anthropology, University of Western Australia. Figures 44 and 45 were taken by Mr. Peter Lucich while he was a research student in the Department of Anthropology, University of Western Australia under a grant from the Australian Institute of Aboriginal Studies: he is now at the Department of Sociology, University of New England, New South Wales.

Some of the figures illustrated here have been produced elsewhere in various other works. The following comments provide some indication of this. Figures 1, 2, 6 and 10 were first published in R. M. Berndt, *Djanggawul*, London, 1952, and Figures 5, 7, 9, 11-12 are similar to those reproduced in that volume. Figure 3 was originally produced in A. P. Elkin, R. M. and C. H. Berndt, *Art in Arnhem Land*, Melbourne, 1950. Figures 15-17 have previously been reproduced in R. M. Berndt, *Kunapipi*, Melbourne, 1951. Part of Figure 25 was reproduced in R. M. and C. H. Berndt, *The World of the First Australians*, Sydney, 1964/68. Figure 26 is similar to one in the last-noted volume and to one in R. M. and C. H. Berndt, *The First Australians*, Sydney, 1952/69. Figures 29 and 31 were also reproduced in C. P. Mountford, *Records of the American-Australian Scientific Expedition to Arnhem Land*, 1, *Art, Myth and Symbolism*, Melbourne, 1956. Paintings similar to those illustrated in Figures 33-36 have been illustrated in I. M. Crawford, *The Art of the Wandjina*, Melbourne, 1968.

Description of the Plates

Figures 1-14 cover the *dua* and *jiridja* moiety *nara* rituals. Figures 1-3*ii*, 4-10 and 14 concern the Djanggawul mytho-ritual cycle. Figures 3*i*, *iii*, and *iv*, 11-14 the Laindjung-Banaidja cycle. Both are relevant to north-eastern Arnhem Land. See this Fascicle, under Fertility Rites.

Figure 1. This is reproduced from a crayon drawing on brown paper by Mawulan, a Riradjingu dialect unit headman at Yirrkalla, 1946-47.

Top panel: from left to right, Bildjiwuraroiju, the elder and Miralaidj the younger of the two Djanggawul sisters, with the Djanggawul brother (right). The Two Sisters have long clitorises and the Brother a long penis; these drag on the ground and resemble *djuda* (tree) *rangga* emblems. They hold goanna tail and *mawulan rangga*, one in each hand: these *rangga* have feathered tassels; the Brother wears a sacred dillybag slung against his chest. From the Two Sisters flow the first people (represented by dots). Between the younger sister and the Brother is a small circle of *rangga* people (who have also emerged from the Mothers), among them the two Wawalag Sisters (see Fascicles One and Two).

Bottom panel: left: Bildjiwuraroiju squats opposite Miralaidj in the posture of child-bearing, hands holding the posts of a hut: feathered tassels hang from their elbows. The Djanggawul Brother has lifted aside their clitorises: people flow out from them, *rangga* males are put on one side, *rangga* females on the other. This mythical event took place at the sacred site of Yawulyawul which marked, traditionally, the western boundary of the north-eastern Arnhem Land cultural bloc. On the right of this panel, the Djanggawul Brother is shown inserting his hand into Miralaidj's vagina and removing the *rangga* people, who are shown flowing from her. *Rangga* emblems (posts) are ranged beside the Brother and Sister. This took place at the sacred site of Dulmulwondeinbi, west of Marabai.

Collected by R. M. Berndt, Yirrkalla, 1946-47.

Figure 2. This is also reproduced from a crayon drawing on brown paper by Mawulan. It is the central panel of a long drawing showing the sacred site of Jelangbara (Yelangbara): see Fascicle Two, Figures 41 to 46.

On the right, bottom, the Djanggawul Brother holds the sacred fringed *ngainmara* conical mat on his thighs: this symbolizes the younger sister, and the conventional position taken in coitus. The *ngainmara* came in the bark canoe from the mythical island of Bralgu (also Land of the *dua* moiety Dead) and contained *rangga* emblems. The Brother, in this illustration, has his hands in the mat and is withdrawing *djuda* and *mawulan rangga* (see also Figure 1: bottom panel, right). Beside and above him are the *rangga* posts with feathered pendants. On the left is the younger sister, and on each side of her the sacred *rangga*. The middle band, with the two *djanda* goanna, represents the sacred shade or shelter. It was at Jelangbara that the Djanggawul first made landfall on the Arnhem Land coast.

Collected by R. M. Berndt, Yirrkalla, 1946-47.

Figure 3. Secret-sacred *rangga*. From left to right:
i   octopus *rangga*, the wool pendants being its tentacles: *jiridja* moiety.
ii Djanggawul Goanna Tail *rangga*: *dua* moiety. See Figure 1.
iii a special tree associated with the Diving Duck: *jiridja* moiety *rangga*, Laindjung-Banaidja cult. See Fascicle One, Figure 9.

iv a coolibah tree which burst into flames at its apex: *jiridja* moiety *rangga*, Laindjung-
   Banaidja cult. See Fascicle One, Figure 14.

   i is of the Waramiri dialect unit. The Dreaming centre of this Octopus (*manda*) is in an
underwater cave in the English Company Islands, Arnhem Land. It is 49.50 inches in
length and was made by Buramara, a Waramiri man now at Elcho Island but then at
Yirrkalla—it is his Dreaming.

   ii has been used in a number of *dua* moiety *nara* rituals, and has been repainted several
times. The ridges at the top are the Goanna's 'shoulders' (or front legs), and it is ridged and
flattened at each side to indicate the Goanna's backbone. The design shows Goanna, and
its tracks and marks on the sand. The whole is bound with jungle twine and hung with
feathered pendants tipped with white eagle-hawk down. It is 52.25 inches in length, and
was made by Mawulan at Yirrkalla.

   iii is associated with the Diving Duck of the Dalwongu dialect unit, in the *jiridja*
moiety Laindjung-Banaidja cycle. It represents the *gwarguma* tree: the bird's head is
carved at the apex and its design under the binding of feathered string symbolizes a
billabong and the splashing of the duck in the water. After diving, in the myth, the bird
perches on this tree: as it shakes itself, a fragment of seaweed falls on its spirit centre at
Gululdji at Blue Mud Bay, in Dalwongu country. The pole is 55.75 inches in length, and
was made by Liagarang, a Dalwongu man (now dead).

   iv also belongs to the Laindjung-Banaidja cycle, of the *jiridja* moiety, and bears the
same designs as on the sacred figure of Laindjung illustrated in Figure 9, Fascicle One. It is
associated with the fire which destroyed the secret-sacred shade: the *rangga* is of the *bunuwa*
Fire Dreaming. The diamond-shaped incising at the apex symbolizes the coolibah tree
bursting into flames. The diamond designs on the trunk refer to ashes from the fire and to
the fire itself. The length of this object is 49.25 inches. It was made by Munggaraui, of the
Gumaidj dialect unit.

   These four *rangga* were obtained at Yirrkalla by R. M. Berndt in 1946-47, and are now
in the Institute of Anatomy Museum, Canberra, having been removed from the Department of Anthropology, University of Sydney.

   Figure 4. The *ngainmara* mat is a sacred object, symbolic of the wombs of the Djanggawul
Sisters, yet it is also utilitarian. This Figure shows an Aboriginal group at Milingimbi
(north-central Arnhem Land), under the tamarind trees originally planted by early
'Macassan' (Indonesian) traders to the north Australian coast. In the central foreground,
a *ngainmara* is in use. On the left is a forked stick from which invocations are ritually
called. Photograph taken in the late 1930's.
   Photo: H. Shepherdson, Elcho Island.

   Figure 5. On the secret-sacred *nara* ritual ground, the Riradjingu headman, Mawulan
(now dead) reveals his Goanna Tail *rangga* (the same object shown in Figure 3, *ii*, above).
Other *rangga* are also displayed.
   Photo: R. M. Berndt, Yirrkalla, 1946-47.

   Figure 6. On the *nara* ground. The tin shack is actually the sacred shade in which the
rangga are stored. Two postulants emerge writhing from the shade, a Goanna Tail *rangga*
resting on their bodies.
   Photo: R. M. Berndt, Yirrkalla, 1946-47.

Figure 7. The two postulants have now emerged: with the Goanna Tail resting upon them, they posture to represent male and female goanna at the sacred site of Jelangbara. The older man is Manimba, a *dua* moiety (Ngeimil dialect unit) ritual leader of the Djang-gawul cult (now dead).

Photo: R. M. Berndt, Yirrkalla, 1946-47.

Figure 8. A further scene in the Goanna ritual, showing the two postulants noted in Figure 7.

Photo: R. M. Berndt, Yirrkalla, 1946-47.

Figure 9. As in Figures 6 to 8: men posturing with the Goanna Tail *rangga*.

Photo: R. M. Berndt, Yirrkalla, 1946-47.

Figure 10. The two postulants shown in Figures 6 to 9 lie together, as male and female goanna, with the Goanna Tail *rangga* upon them: final scene.

Photo: R. M. Berndt, Yirrkalla, 1946-47.

Figure 11. Postulants of the *jiridja* moiety dance outside the sacred shade on the *nara* ground. The figure on the right, Birigidji, a Dalwongu ritual leader of the Laindjung-Banaidja cult, is calling the invocations before the emergence of the *rangga*. Postulants are decorated on their chests with the fire-and-ashes patterns noted in Figure 3, *iv*, and are similar to those on the carved figure of the mythic being Laindjung—see Fascicle One, Figure 9.

Photo: R. M. Berndt, Yirrkalla, 1946-47.

Figure 12. The *jiridja* moiety fire-and-ashes *rangga* is held in dancing before the *nara* shade. Liagarang, Dalwongu dialect unit, holds the *rangga*.

Photo: R. M. Berndt, Yirrkalla, 1946-47.

Figure 13. Invocations are called, to the accompaniment of clapping-sticks, by the ritual leader, Birigidji. The top of the *rangga* is visible in the centre.

Photo: R. M. Berndt, Yirrkalla, 1946-47.

Figure 14. The final scene of the *dua* and *jiridja* moiety *nara* rituals, in which members of both moieties (as separate groups, as shown) immerse themselves in the sea. This is done partly for ritual purification, but also because the Djanggawul themselves were stained with sea water after their mythic voyage from the island of Bralgu. All members of the camp participate in this ritual act.

Photo: H. Shepherdson, Milingimbi, late 1930's.

Figures 15 to 25 refer to the Kunapipi Fertility cult. The mythology this ritual sequence relates to concerns the two Wawalag Sisters—see annotations to Figures in Fascicle One, especially Figure 8 and in Fascicle Two, Figures 20 to 25.

In this Fascicle, Figures 15 to 17 are drawings in lumber crayon on brown paper obtained at Yirrkalla in 1946-47. These were prepared by Gumug of the Dalwongu dialect unit, *jiridja* moiety.

Figure 15. This depicts postulants and novices in a ritual performance on the *kunapipi* ground. At left centre, is the *darlba* snake as a *jelmalandji* structure erected at the *nanggaru* pit (centre) from which rises a further *jelmalandji* representing the *gundaru* Lightning Snake: both are Yulunggul, and both are topped with feathered ornaments. On the left of the *jelmalandji* is a boomerang-shaped trench, the *ganala*, with a row of *jiridja* moiety novices on its concave side; along the track leading to the *ganala* are *dua* moiety novices. On the extreme left is a row of postulants: three 'male possum' dancers with long paperbark penes, and below them three 'female possums' and two 'male possums'. In the top section, above the *nanggaru* and the horizontally placed *jelmalandji*, are *jiridja* moiety men who have prepared the *jelmalandji* for the *dua* moiety participants. Within the *nanggaru*, possum dancers move round, entering the central circle symbolizing the sacred billabong. These men emerge from the *nanggaru* and cover it with dancing feet. Below (right, under *nanggaru* and *jelmalandji*), dance male and female possum actors.

Obtained by R. M. Berndt at Yirrkalla, 1946-47.

Figure 16. This drawing is divided into two panels. On the left is the *nanggaru* (centre) with a Galerigalering mythic spirit above it, wearing a conical headdress tipped with feathers. He is dancing for the spirits of the Wawalag Sisters who have been swallowed by Yulunggul. On his left (arranged horizontally) are two actors representing him; one holds green branches, the other a boomerang. Below them are *jiridja* moiety novices. Beside the *nanggaru* (below) are three actors with a bullroarer between them; they are performing a pandanus ritual, which is being shown to novices. A large *jelmalandji* stands nearby, bearing the Yulunggul design. Above the *nanggaru* are four *dua* moiety novices and four *jiridja* moiety youths and men who are seeing the *kunapipi* for the first time (as 'advanced novices'). Beside the *jelmalandji* and the right hand panel is the row of 'advanced novices' (the same as above; they have 'moved over'); one of them, as a headman, clapping his sticks and singing.

The right hand panel shows the *ganala* trench: at top left are novices watching ritual possum dancing by men moving down the track leading to the *ganala*. The long row, from top to bottom left of the right hand panel, comprises novices under the branches of the *djebalmandji*: at each end sit the *jiridja* moiety guardians, calling out. Below the *nanggaru* dances a man representing the Blue-tongue Lizard. The *jelmalandji*, with its Yulunggul decoration, stands upright: on its left, a row of men dance round the *ganala*, their leader beating his clapping-sticks (bottom); and on the right, a further row of men perform the cabbage palm dancing.

Obtained by R. M. Berndt at Yirrkalla, 1946-47.

Figure 17. The main subject of this drawing is concerned primarily with ritual coitus on the *kunapipi* ground.

The top panel depicts the sacred boomerang, around which the actual and classificatory brothers of the women having coitus (in the top row) stand facing away from them, since brothers should conventionally avoid all recognition of their sisters' behaviour in this respect. The women have coitus with men to whom they normally stand in an avoidance relationship. In the middle is a row of men awaiting their turn.

In the bottom panel are the *jelmalandji* and the *nanggaru*. The former is held by one man (right), with a row of dancing men (feet to *jelmalandji*) who are the actual or classificatory husbands of the women having coitus: these men await their turn with women who are the wives (actual and classificatory) of men shown in the top panel. These women are having coitus (bottom, right), while three men wait. On the other side of the *jelmalandji*, men perform the possum dance round the *nanggaru*: they are fathers (actual and classificatory) of both groups of women.

Obtained by R. M. Berndt at Yirrkalla, 1946-47.

Figure 18. This illustrates a small *jelmalandji*, built up on a sheet of bark. The central figure is Yulunggul (in red-ochre), against a background of white 'wool' stuck on to the bark with blood. Emu feathers are at the apex. It is either placed at the *nanggaru* or used as a headdress. The large *jelmalandji*, illustrated in Figures 15 to 17, usually range from twelve to over twenty feet in height: this one is about three feet in height.

Obtained by R. M. Berndt at Yirrkalla, 1946-47. Now in the collection of the Department of Anthropology, University of Western Australia.

Figure 19. This shows a number of men twirling bullroarers for a *kunapipi* ritual. At Milingimbi, north-central Arnhem Land, during the late 1930's.

Photo: H. Shepherdson, Elcho Island.

Figure 20. The secret-sacred *kunapipi* ground. In the clearing is the *nanggaru*; in the background the two *jelmalandji* structures, with their meandering snake designs, stand by the *ganala*. One represents the Yulunggul Rock Python, the other a cabbage palm. At Milingimbi, during the late 1930's.

Photo: H. Shepherdson, Elcho Island.

Figure 21. On the *kunapipi* ground, at the tapering end of the ground where the shade has been erected. This represents the place where the Wawalag sheltered at the sacred site of Muruwul. The long *yulunggul* didjeridu is being blown: this represents the Rock Python: the end of the instrument is being held up by a posturing goanna man (see design on his chest). The *yulunggul* will later be played over a row of novices to symbolize their being swallowed as the Wawalag were. At Milingimbi, during the late 1930's.

Photo: H. Shepherdson, Elcho Island.

Figure 22. On the *kunapipi* ground, where a pit has been dug. This is at Oenpelli, in western Arnhem Land, where the pit is called *ganala* although the more correct term *nanggaru* is also used for it. Mounds of sand surround it, and on its walls is etched the Python design, but also, in this area, the Ngaljod, as Rainbow Snake and Mother. It represents the womb of the Mother.

Photo: R. M. Berndt, Oenpelli, 1950.

Figure 23. A postulant in the *kunapipi* ritual. He wears a feather-down design (stuck on with blood) of Ngaljod, the Rainbow Snake, and her eggs.

Photo: R. M. Berndt, Oenpelli, 1950.

Figure 24. Men from the secret-sacred *kunapipi* ground assemble round the forked *djebalmandji*, before the ritual leaders climb it to call sacred invocations. At Milingimbi, during the late 1930's.

Photo: H. Shepherdson, Elcho Island.

Figure 25. Men, after returning from the secret-sacred *kunapipi* ground, surround women who are crouched beneath *ngainmara* conical mats and blankets. Older women, who are not covered, call the names of foods forbidden to women at this time. At Milingimbi, during the late 1930's.

Photo: H. Shepherdson, Elcho Island.

Figure 26. Painting a prospective novice for the western Arnhem Land *maraiin* rituals. The body painting is done in ochres, with designs representing crocodile tongue and kangaroo (highly conventionalized).

Photo: R. M. Berndt, Oenpelli, 1950.

Figure 27. Ritual *maraiin* dancing outside the *jiridja* moiety shade. The participants, under the direction of the leader who sings and beats time with this clapping-sticks, are dancing in the same way as did the mythic being Laradjeidja.

Photo: R. M. Berndt, Oenpelli, 1950.

Figure 28. *Jiridja* moiety men emerging from the sacred shade to the accompaniment of clapping-sticks. They writhe on the ground, one behind the other, the first holding a sacred *maraiin* object (fire).

Photo: R. M. Berndt, Oenpelli, 1950.

Figures 29 to 32 are from Groote Eylandt, and show excerpts from the Amunduwuraria rituals. These focus on varying anthropomorphic beings or mythic spirits and closely resemble some aspects of the north-eastern Arnhem Land *nara* rituals.

Figure 29. The opening dance. Postulants walk up and down the secret-sacred ground, dragging their feet in the sand. This ground represents a river created by Aidja, a Rainbow Snake or serpent, and the men are painted with the design of this mythic creature.

Photo: C. P. Mountford, Groote Eylandt, 1948.

Figure 30. A postulant representing the fresh-water Tortoise (*jumununda*) who travelled inland to Wurindi (near Bennett Bay) on the mainland, a place also associated with Aidja: Tortoise was searching for a waterhole. The performer postures as the names of sacred waterholes are invoked.

Photo: C. P. Mountford, Groote Eylandt, 1948.

Figure 31. Participants performing the Crab dance (*unwala*), one of a number of dances in this series.

Photo: C. P. Mountford, Groote Eylandt, 1948.

Figure 32. This scene represents the dance of the mythic Bandicoots (*banguruk*) who lived at Wurindi and are associated with Aidja. Behind the 'barrier' of singing men with clapping-sticks a bandicoot actor crawls on the sand, his arms spread forward with a ritual object representing its tongue (not seen) held in his mouth.

Photo: C. P. Mountford, Groote Eylandt, 1948.

Figures 33 to 36 illustrate Wondjina (Wandjina) paintings from the Kimberley region of Western Australia. See this Fascicle.

Figure 33. Wondjina at Mamadai, near the Durack River. An Aboriginal is re-touching the paintings. The name of this Wondjina is Morol: behind these figures a kangaroo is painted, but is not clearly visible in this illustration. Morol chased this animal, which climbed the hill at Mamadai—following it, he cornered it and called the place by this name, and put the painting there.

Photo: I. M. Crawford, Western Australian Museum, 1966.

Figure 34. An extension of the Wondjina painting at Mamadai illustrated in Figure 33. Here the buttocks of the kangaroo are more clearly seen behind and between the two middle Wondjina.

Photo: I. M. Crawford, Western Australian Museum, 1966.

Figure 35. Walamud and other Wondjina at the western end of the cave at Wanalirri, located near Mamadai, not far from the Gibb River pastoral station; it is really a rock shelter at the bottom of a high cliff in a gorge.

Photo: I. M. Crawford, Western Australian Museum, 1966.

Figure 36. The mythic being Kaiara, similar to the Wondjina associated with wind, rain and lightning, and responsible for sending out spirit children: these Kaiara were brought to the mainland by a whirlwind from the sea, and are said to be able to bring lightning by blinking their eyes. This particular example is from Chalangdal, on Vansittart Bay, north-west of Kalumburu mission settlement.

Photo: I. M. Crawford, Western Australian Museum, 1963.

Figures 37 to 43 constitute a small series from Kununurra Aboriginal reserve, in the Ord River area of the Kimberleys, Western Australia.

Figure 37. Sacred objects being removed from Ivanhoe pastoral station: they were stored in a specially prepared repository, a bough shelter, placed on a platform and protected from rain and direct sunshine by sheets of iron. The Aborigines involved are Miriwong.

Photo: B. Shaw, Kununurra. 1970.

Figure 38. A typical rock shelter, used for storing sacred materials.
Photo: B. Shaw, Kununurra, 1970.

Figure 39. The same rock shelter shown in Figure 38: a sacred board is being placed in it.
Photo: B. Shaw, Kununurra, 1970.

Figure 40. Four sacred boards on display, after removal from their repository. These boards belong to the *gurangara* cult associated with the mythic being Djanba. See H. Petri, *Sterbende Welt in Nordwestaustralien*, 1954, and A. Lommel, *Die Unambal*, 1952. Such boards are held and danced with on the secret-sacred ground.

Photo: B. Shaw, Kununurra, 1970.

Figure 41. A non-secret object called *wurangu* (string cross or thread cross, similar to the Desert *wanigi*: See Fascicle Four, Chapter Five, under The Iconographic Context), associated with a dance-cycle called *balga* which originally came from Derby. The *wurangu* is being constructed at Kununurra by three men from Fork Creek, near Wyndham, who use a wood frame and wool twine. In dancing, it is carried on the back of a participant. Such objects were previously secret-sacred, but are now said (in this area) to represent the mast of a sailing ship.

Photo: B. Shaw, Kununurra, 1970.

Figure 42. On the ground lies a completed *wurangu* (string cross). Held upright is a long board used in the *balga* dancing, which has at its apex a small *wurangu*. Its design represents camping places (hills, waterholes, etc.), with a central figure of a spirit frog; on the opposite side (not seen) is a human figure. This is probably associated with 'outside' (public) versions of the Djanba myth.

Photo: B. Shaw, Kununurra, 1970.

Figure 43. A circle of *balga* participants and singers complete the song-sequence. The majority are from Fork Creek, near Wyndham, but they include two Miriwong and Gadjerong men.

Photo: B. Shaw, Kununurra, 1970.

Figure 44. Typical dancing at Kalumburu mission settlement in the northern Kimberleys. Such dances are non-secret and are held in the main camp. However, they do have a religious flavour, and are said to have been influenced from the east—which is in the direction of the Port Keats area of the Northern Territory. In this illustration, the dance is about a fishing line, and is relevant to a myth.

Photo: P. Lucich, Kalumburu, 1963.

Figure 45. A typical traditional dance sequence of Djanba (mythic being) affinity, performed by older men in the main camp—a public performance. Such dances dramatize various natural species, and are often derived from a dream experienced by the leader.

Photo: P. Lucich, Kalumburu, 1963.

PLATES

PLATES

1. A drawing of the sacred Djanggawul myth. The Two Sisters give birth to the first people. *Rangga* emblems are also depicted. Yirrkalla, Arnhem Land.

2. A drawing of the sacred Djanggawul myth. Sacred *vangga* are removed from the conical mat. Yirrkalla, Arnhem Land.

3. Secret-sacred *rangga*. From left to right: Octopus (*jiridja* moiety);
Djanggawul Goanna Tail (*dua* moiety); Diving Duck tree (*jiridja*
moiety); and a coolibah tree relevant to Laindjung-Banaidja
(*jiridja*) moiety. Yirrkalla, Arnhem Land.

4. A sacred conical mat (*ngainmara*) in use. Milingimbi, Arnhem Land.

5. *Dua* moiety *nara* rituals. Revealing the Goanna Tail *rangga* of the Djanggawul. Yirrkalla, Arnhem Land.

6. *Dua* moiety *nara* rituals. Two postulants emerge from sacred hut on secret-sacred ground. Yirrkalla, Arnhem Land.

7. *Dua* moiety *nara* rituals. Two postulants with sacred Goanna Tail *rangga* resting on them. Yirrkalla, Arnhem Land.

8. *Dua* moiety *nara* rituals. A scene from the Goanna ritual of the Djanggawul. Yirrkalla, Arnhem Land.

9. *Dua moiety nara rituals.* Men posturing with Goanna Tail *rangga.* Yirrkalla, Arnhem Land.

10. *Dua* moiety *nara* rituals. Two postulants lie together, as male and female Goanna, with Goanna Tail *rangga* on them. Yirrkalla, Arnhem Land.

11. *Jiridja* moiety *nara* rituals. Dancing outside the sacred hut: calling invocations, in the Laindjung-Banaidja series. Yirrkalla, Arnhem Land.

12. *Jiridja* moiety *nara* rituals. The fire-and-ashes *rangga* is held in dancing. Yirrkalla, Arnhem Land.

13. *Jiridja* moiety *nara* rituals. Calling the invocations, while holding the *rangga*. Yirrkalla, Arnhem Land.

14. Final scene in *dua* and *jiridja* moiety *nara* rituals: immersion in the sea. Milingimbi, Arnhem Land.

15. *Kunapipi* ritual. Drawing of postulants and novices, showing *jelmalandji, ganala* and *nanggaru,* with ritual dancing. Yirrkalla, Arnhem Land.

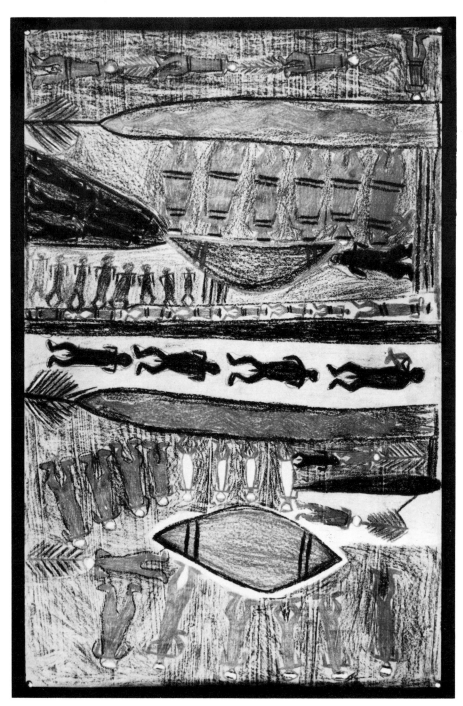

16. *Kunapipi* ritual. Drawing of postulants and novices, showing *jelmalandji, nanggaru, ganala* and *djebalmandji,* with ritual dancing. Yirrkalla, Arnhem Land.

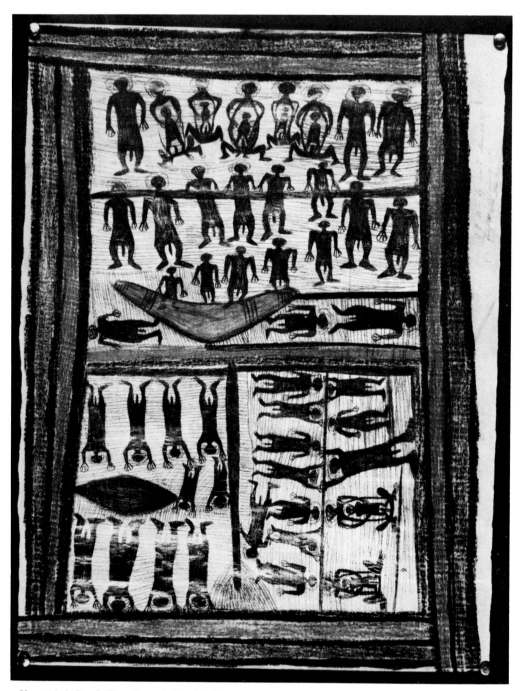

17. *Kunapipi* ritual. Drawing of ritual coitus on the secret-sacred ground. Yirrkalla, Arnhem Land.

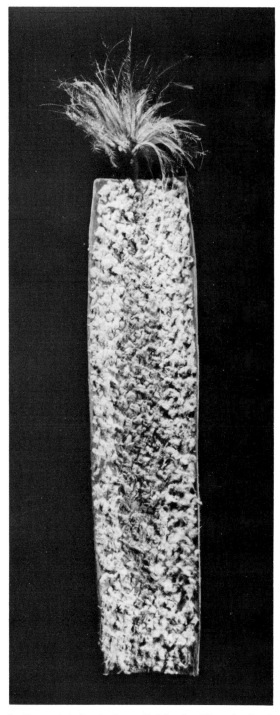

18. *Kunapipi* ritual. A small *jelmalandji* on bark, the
design in wild cotton. Yirrkalla, Arnhem Land.

19. *Kunapipi* ritual. Men twirling bullroarers. Milingimbi, Arnhem Land.

20. *Kunapipi* ritual. The *nanggaru* and two *jelma-landji* on the secret-sacred ground. Milingimbi, Arnhem Land.

21. *Kunapipi* ritual. Blowing the Yulunggul didjeridu on the *kunapipi* ground, before a posturing Goanna man. Milingimbi, Arnhem Land.

22. The *ganala* or *nanggaru* pit at Oenpelli (Arnhem Land) during *kunapipi* rituals: Python or Ngaljod

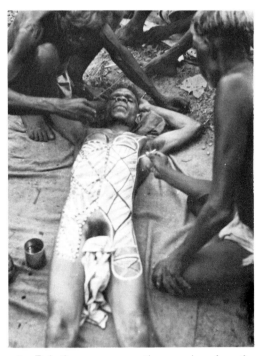

23. *Kunapipi* ritual. A postulant decorated with a design of Rainbow Snake and eggs. Oenpelli, Arnhem Land.

26. Painting a prospective novice for the western Arnhem Land *maraiin* rituals. Oenpelli.

27. Ritual *maraiin* dancing outside the *jiridja* moiety shade. Oenpelli, Arnhem Land.

24. *Kunapipi* ritual. Assembling round forked *djebalmandji* before ritual leaders climb it to call sacred invocations. Milingimbi, Arnhem Land.

25. *Kunapipi* ritual. Men returning from secret-sacred ground surround women covered with conical mats and blankets. Milingimbi, Arnhem Land.

28. *Jiridja* moiety men emerge from the sacred *maraiin* shade. Oenpelli, Arnhem Land.

29. Amunduwuraria rituals, Groote Eylandt. Postulants walk up and down the secret-sacred ground representing a river made by Aidja, a Rainbow Snake.

30. Amunduwuraria rituals, Groote Eylandt. Postulant representing fresh water Tortoise.

31. Amunduwuraria rituals, Groote Eylandt. Participants performing
Crab dance.

32. Amunduwuraria rituals, Groote Eylandt. Dance of the mythic Bandicoots.

33. Wondjina cave paintings, Kimberleys. Wondjina paintings at Mamadai: being re-touched.

34. Wondjina cave paintings, Kimberleys. Wondjina paintings at Mamadai.

35. Wondjina cave paintings, Kimberleys. Walamud and other Wondjina at Wanalirri.

36. Wondjina cave paintings, Kimberleys. The mythic being Kaiara, associated with wind, rain and lightning, and responsible for sending out spirit children.

37. Kununurra series, Kimberleys. Sacred objects removed from their repository.

38. Kununurra series, Kimberleys. A rock shelter used for storing sacred materials.

39. Kununurra series, Kimberleys. A sacred board is placed in the rock shelter.

40. Kununurra series, Kimberleys. Displaying sacred boards belonging to the *gurangara* cult associated with the mythic being Djanba.

41. Kununurra series, Kimberleys. *Wurangu* thread-cross associated with the *balga* dance cycle.

42. Kununurra series, Kimberleys. The completed *wurangu* (on the ground)
and the long board (upright) for *balga* dancing. It is probably
associated with the Djanba myth.

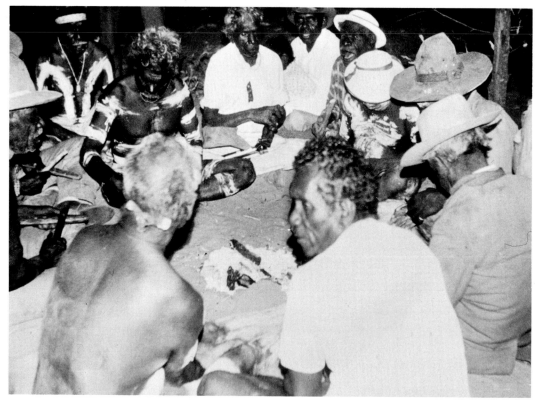

43. Kununurra series, Kimberleys. A circle of *balga* participants and singers complete a song-sequence.

44. Typical dancing at Kalumburu, Kimberleys, dramatizing a mythical event concerning a fishing line.

45. A traditional dance sequence of Djanba affinity. Kalumburu, Kimberleys.